Selected Poems
1970 – 1980

Nancy Muller

Illustrated by Shelby Faircloth

Dedication

I grew up on a cattle farm in South Carolina, where my father was born and raised. This environment stimulated my imagination about the personalities of living creatures, as well as inanimate objects such as favorite dolls and "stuffies," serving as my companions because we were so remotely removed from friends and relatives.

I don't recall precisely when first formally exposed to poetry to begin composing poems of my own. It was undoubtedly when attending an all-girls school in Charleston, SC. All twelve poems herein surfaced over the decade to follow, when hundreds more were written, as I completed my schooling and began working in New York City.

Now as a grandmother, I am eager to share some of my most treasured writings first and foremost with my grandchildren. I have more to share as they grow older. Still, this first published collection is selected especially for them and thus dedicated to them.

Such a creation could not have been possible without a most wonderful and creative artist to illustrate the creatures and feelings housed in this waterfall of words. Equal credit for this publication therefore belongs to Shelby Faircloth as interpreter and illustrator, with whom I am proud to be associated. I am also grateful for the cover design and layout talents of Stephanee Killen, poet, entrepreneur, author and Integrative Ink owner.

With love to all my readers,

Cabell on a Sunday

Across the thin bridge
        between my stiff world
        of soiled grown-up-ness
        and his, springing crisp,
the laugh of a child
gently echoes through
        hushed, winding breezes
        where early secrets
        of innocence sleep.

I faintly hear tunes
in the afternoon
            and listen for songs
            that my soul once sang
            with a glad rhythm
            only children sing.

Now the memory
of youth's jubilee
        serves to anchor me
        to recollections
        in solemnity.

Clearview Plantation

Go home to your farm ……

      lie down and breathe in
      the summer season
         filling soft pastures
         with the red clover
         your spirit fed on
         for twenty-five years.

Sink, as in goose down
      chocolated with dew,
      and doze to Mozart
         in the wooded shade
         by a favorite lake
         near the white framed house
         above it hillside
         to hear the red-wing
         blackbird chirp the tune.

Go back ……

      It's time to return
      and renew yourself
      for the years to come.

And when swinging in
      the wooden grapevine,
      a familiar harp,
         call for me to come
         with spaniel at side
         and I will join you.

Of Gentle Laughter

Children skate over cracking walks,
Dogs nip wheels of those being taught.

What the morning has brought to light
Is but a journey into night,
Of gentle laughter
        Of placid rushes
                Of silver moonbeams:

A life too luscious
For words from a pen
Trying to capture
My childhood again.

Royal Garden

I am greeted by the hustle
and bustle of my spring garden,
and although it is difficult
to say "good day" - a mere "hello" -
apparently my "neighbors" know
I've come to visit for a while.

Blades of grass bow, as palace guards,
when I pass…..
                    Did I hear a laugh?
Or was it the chuckling of oaks
tickled by a mischievous breeze
dancing among glistening green leaves
Or a grey squirrel cracking a shell,
diving into his storage bins,
too anxious for winter to come.

I can't disclose to you for sure ---
as the sounds fully integrate
like instruments in a Bach suite:
each with its own distinctive voice,
when one player alone would lack
what's necessary to the whole.

And I, the queen of these creatures,
Am blessed to know all their features.

The Oak Outside My Bedroom Window

A handsome chipmunk whispered in my ear –

What did I hear?
"Come dance with me and we shall play,
skipping and giggling the live-long day.
And when the evening sun glows in nocturnal approach,
we'll nestle heads in a soft bed within my coach
stationed in the hospitable arms
of Mr. Oak's unfailing charm."

So follow I did:
How we scampered to the rhythm
of heartbeats protected by dreams
coming true to us so it seemed.

Our thoughts scampered along those beams
stretching forth mightily beneath
unpredictable pattering
of tiny feet.

The love for one to another
and the playhouse that we cherished
radiated to the heavens
a supreme passion for living,
pronouncing unconquerable will
to fly away on strong branches
from today until tomorrow
and still further.

Carousel Ride

Imagining self
        in fierce steeple chase,
    painted steed and me
        glide upward embraced.

A carousel host
        of all who embrace
    chance costing a dime
        points out the staircase
    up to stars we'll climb.

Circus ground motions
        are left behind cold
    as we pass meteors
        of light to behold.

Release emotions,
        soar celestial heights,
    get ten minutes' worth
        of bliss for the night.

Complete loss of depth,
        hearing, taste, and sight
    renders feeling sole
        pilot of this flight.

Nadia

A spry shimmering
sparkle of youth's strength
twirls her way among
gazing spectators
spellbound by the grace
of her slender legs
and firm quick torso
as her back handsprings
and successive flips
allow us viewers
to seize her salto
as seamless streaming
leaps with precision
of form in landing
her feet followed by
a split without pause
until a rapid tuck
sends her in dismount
faster than the keys
of a light-hearted
piano scherzo.

Tranced we watch her fly.

Pawn of Daybreak

sparrow
        such a pawn of daybreak he is
        continues to cheep and chitter
glad songs
        that we have dawned another day
to live.

poor slave
        never granted brief vacation
        or pledged human adoration
he stands
        perched ready draped in dull brown dress
to sing.

        never does he fail to greet sun
        or bid adieu to waning moon.

a giant
        he is in his own chipper way
        rarely noticed in hidden queue
        a first soprano in God's choir
no less.

Our Sound of Autumn

Parading laughter
        comes prancing across
        lightly moistened leaves
                painted vermillion
                and robed in gold fleece.

A scampering step
        brings both of us through
        the deep beds of hues
                christened by frost's reign
                over maple woods.

And conversation
        between us dances
        wildly in between
                trees inhabited
                just by you and me
                        with our voices' ring
                        but stilled by being.

                The silence is one
                only we can hear.

My Favorite Stuffies

A monkey's laughter rings….
      oh, it must be Charlie's….
            better yet, Rita's shrill….
we're having but the best
of fun lying in bed
tickling one another
with midnight tales' delight.

Two handsome pillow mates
are truly what they are….
      no rebuttals nor scorn
         just comforting, soft love.

One world is what
we breathe into,
      as dreams carry
      the all of us
            from bed chambers
            to morning play.

Daffodil's Laughter

Daffodil -
      lazily grinning
      swishing hips from
      side to side
      in breezes tickling
      her yellow collars
      of pastel satin -

I walk and pick
      as if I thought
      the beauty in hand
      could and should become
      a part of me.

Glowing yolk treasures
      can cajole a soul
      into believing
      transfiguration
      is so easy.

It's more than a touch
or plucking from the earth.

Her laughter rules over us all.

My Reply to You

flitting   flirting   firefly
streak your rhinestoned wingspan
across my tired shoulders
so I might share in
the silver transience
of nocturnal flight by
that lithe, weightless body.

Desiring a moment
of magical rhythms
to stroke my eager limbs,
I wait and hold my breath
to feel the waltz of your
radiance over me.

Seven times seventy
years away from waking,
I bask in your glitter,
wishful for tinseled touch
as a sweet reminder
that you are near for now
then with a flash gone yet
only once more returned
until night draws its end.

About the Author

Nancy Muller was born in Houston. At the age of five, her family moved to South Carolina to the farm where her father was born and raised. Nancy's grandfather had managed this land as a dairy farmer, but her father converted it to beef cattle upon moving his own family there from Texas.

After attending local and nearby schools, Nancy chose to attend boarding school in Charleston, SC and graduated from Ashley Hall in 1971, to be welcomed afterwards by Duke University from which she graduated in 1974. While enrolled at Duke, she studied abroad in Aix-en-Provence and traveled throughout Europe from her base in France. After completing her MBA at the Darden School of the University of Virginia, Nancy worked for 15 years for W. R. Grace & Co. before entering the health care sector.

Having earned her PhD in health services research at Virginia Commonwealth University, she was hired by the College of Charleston, from which she retired as visiting associate professor to be closer to her grandchildren living in the Boston area. Nancy and her husband moved to Massachusetts in 2021. Since then, she has become bi-coastal to spend time with another grandchild living in the Santa Barbara environs.

Selected Poems 1970 – 1980 is her first published book.

About the Illustrator

Shelby Faircloth is an illustrator of children's books including Kristen Goldie Huber's *Little Liberty's I Love America*, AB Barnes's *Farmer Fred and the Missing Duckling*, and Kat McKenzie's *Olive and Fae* series. Her love of flora and fauna inspires her style of watercolors to be soft and playful. Shelby lives in Maryland's tidewater country with her family and two precious Havanese.